Hanni and Beth
SAFE & SOUND

Written by Beth Finke

Illustrated by
Anthony Alex LeTourneau

Hanni and Beth: Safe & Sound
Published by Blue Marlin Publications

Text copyright © 2007 by Beth Finke
Illustrations copyright © 2007 by Anthony Alex LeTourneau

Blue Marlin Publications, Ltd.
823 Aberdeen Road, West Bay Shore, NY 11706
www.bluemarlinpubs.com

Printed and bound in China by Regent Publishing Services, Ltd.
Book design & layout by Anthony Alex LeTourneau

Library of Congress Cataloging-in-Publication Data

Finke, Beth, 1958-
 Hanni and Beth : safe & sound / story by Beth Finke ; illustrations by Anthony Alex LeTourneau.
    p. cm.
 ISBN 978-0-9792918-0-7 (hardcover : alk. paper) -- ISBN 978-0-9792918-1-4 (softcover : alk. paper)
 1. Finke, Beth, 1958---Juvenile literature.   2. Hanni (Dog) [proposed]--Juvenile literature.
 3. Guide dogs--United States--Juvenile literature.   4. Guide dogs--Training of--Morristown--New Jersey--Juvenile literature.   I. LeTourneau, Anthony Alex.   II. Title.

 HV1780.F56 2007
 362.4'183--dc22

                            2007003741

Blue Marlin Publications, Ltd.
823 Aberdeen Road, West Bay Shore, NY 11706
www.bluemarlinpubs.com

First printing 2007

To Randy Cox, a special man who loves a special Seeing Eye dog.

To Don Miller and Pastor Matt Chandler, whose teachings help others
to truly see.

Look at me! See the harness strapped to my back? I'm called a Seeing Eye dog. The harness is my uniform, and whenever I'm wearing it, I'm working. I guide my partner, Beth, where she needs to go.

Beth is blind. She can't see, even when her eyes are open. She holds my harness when we leave home. Guiding Beth is my job, and I love it.

I slip us past garbage cans, between tables at outdoor cafes, and around holes in the sidewalk. Thanks to me, Beth doesn't crash. Or bump. Or fall down. I watch for traffic, too. That's the most important part of my job–keeping us safe.

We live in a busy city. I pay close attention when I'm working. When my harness is on, I don't stop to eat. Or sniff. Or even roll over to scratch my back. I do all that at home before Beth straps on my harness, or after she takes it off at night.

Beth works, too. She's a writer. We travel together to all sorts of places-government meetings, award ceremonies, music concerts, and baseball games. Beth writes about interesting people. Like politicians. And professors. And musicians. And baseball grounds keepers. Everywhere Beth goes, I go. I help keep her safe.

And Beth gives me a warm, happy home that always smells good! Especially when she's baking her famous breads! We make a great team.

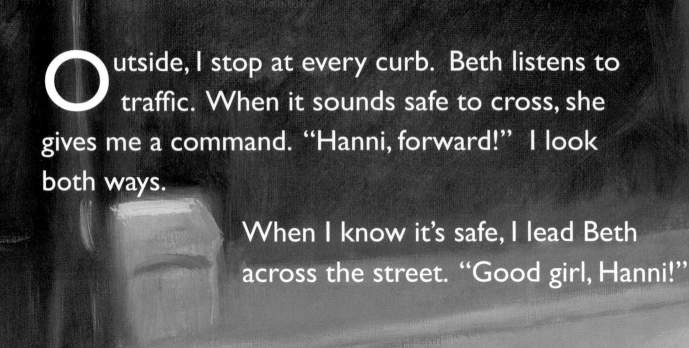

Outside, I stop at every curb. Beth listens to traffic. When it sounds safe to cross, she gives me a command. "Hanni, forward!" I look both ways.

When I know it's safe, I lead Beth across the street. "Good girl, Hanni!"

There have been times when I have had to disobey Beth's commands because she would not have been safe. One time, she didn't know there was a hole in the sidewalk. She urged me to go forward, but I wouldn't listen. "Good girl, Hanni! Good girl!" Keeping us safe is the most important thing I do.

I like people, but they shouldn't pet or talk to me while I'm working. That way, I can pay close attention to Beth. That way, we'll be safe.

I am proud to work at my job every day, and happy to be allowed places where most dogs can't go. Sometimes, though, I wish I didn't have to work. Other dogs get to fetch balls and visit with dog friends while they take walks. I can't even stop to empty (that's a nice word for pee and poop) unless Beth takes off my harness and says, "Park time!"

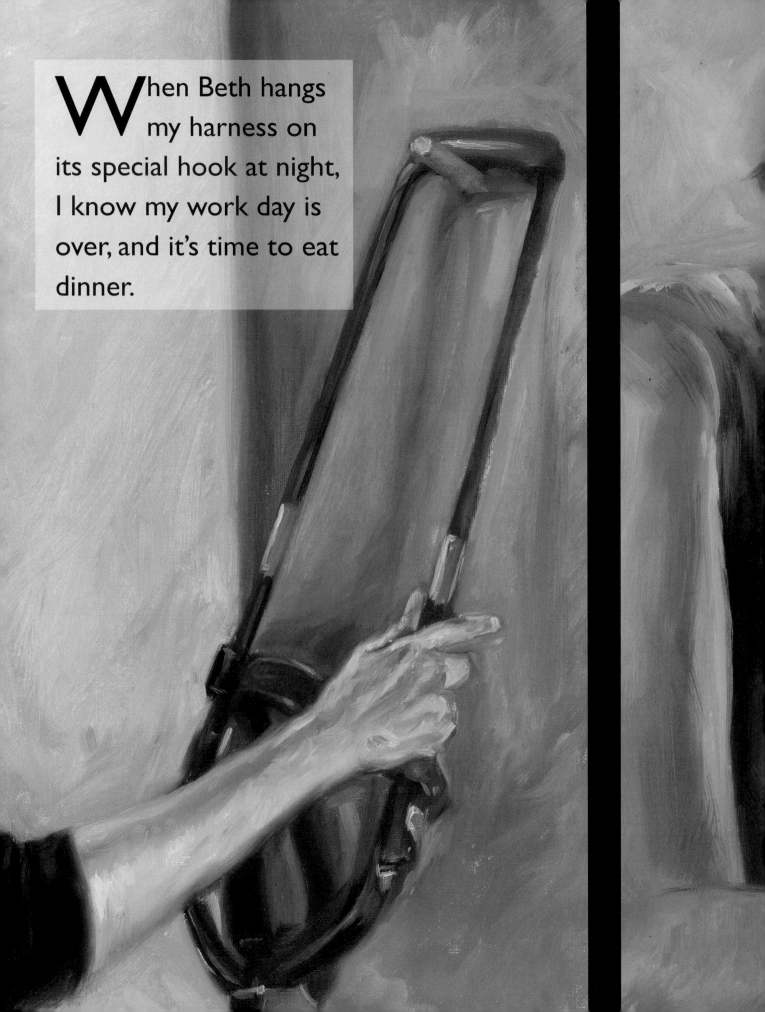

When Beth hangs my harness on its special hook at night, I know my work day is over, and it's time to eat dinner.

And play!

When it's time for bed, Beth brushes me, pets me in my favorite spot, and gives me a treat. "Thanks for all your help today, Hanni. I love you. Goodnight!"

And then I remember how important my job is and how special I am. Goodnight, Beth! I love you, too. And don't worry, Beth. I'll keep us safe tomorrow. And every day after that.

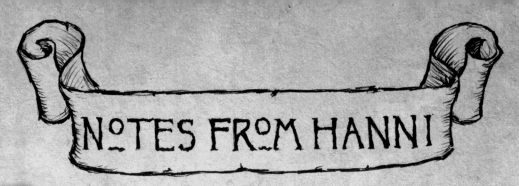

NOTES FROM HANNI

It took a lot of schooling for me to learn my job. I was even born at a school: the Seeing Eye school in Morristown, New Jersey. I stayed at the school with my mama and brothers and sisters for eight weeks. Then a family came to take me to their house for a while. They were volunteers, called puppy raisers.

My time with the puppy raisers was like preschool. They taught me all the basic commands.

Sit. Stay. Normal dog stuff.

A special scarf around my neck set me apart as a puppy in training. The puppy raisers took me everywhere, including the bathroom stall at the library. I even went on a ferris wheel once! They trained me to feel comfortable in all sorts of places. And with all kinds of people.

When I turned one-and-a-half, the puppy raisers took me back to the school where I was born. I had to take a lot of tests before being accepted into the training program. Not all the puppies make it past this stage. They get adopted by families instead.

But I was determined. I wanted to be a Seeing Eye dog. Was I strong enough? Healthy? A good learner? Confident? Yes! I held my head high when I passed the tests and traded my scarf for a harness. But my head wasn't always high during the months I spent learning to guide Beth.

School was very hard. A trainer taught me to stop at stairs, or when something was in the way. I learned a lot of commands, like left, right, and forward. Some days, I just wanted to be goofing around like other dogs. One time, I even crashed my trainer into a tree. I was so busy looking at a barking dog inside a house that I forgot to pay attention to where we were going.

"Phooey!" the trainer exclaimed, pointing to the tree to remind me not to run into it. "Let's try that again." We reversed our steps. This time I focused on my work and avoided the tree. My trainer was much happier. "Good dog, Hanni!"

After I trained for four months, Beth arrived at the school. As always, I tried my best to behave and do as I was told. Beth and I practiced different walking routes through Morristown, New Jersey for three weeks. She learned to trust me to keep her safe, and I learned to trust her to feed me. And give me water. And take me outside four times a day to empty. Remember-- empty is a nice word we use for pee and poop. Beth and I spent every minute of every hour of every day together at the school. At night, she even looped my leash around her bedpost, so I'd be close to her while we slept. The more I got to know Beth, the more I liked her. And the more I wanted to keep her safe.

Soon, Beth took me to her home in Chicago for good. She took me on my first airplane! I knew Beth and I were a team now.

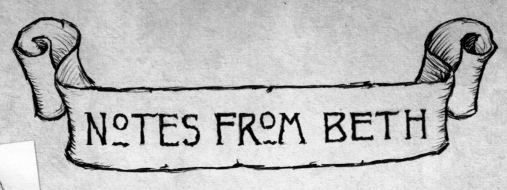

NOTES FROM BETH

I wasn't born blind. I could see when I was a little girl. When I grew up, I became blind from a medical condition called diabetes. It was hard to walk around without tripping over things or bumping into walls and hurting myself. I always had to hold onto someone else. But everyone likes to do things alone sometimes. It makes us proud to do things by ourselves. So I went to a special school for people who are blind. A teacher showed me how to wave a cane in front of me when I walk. That way the cane would run into things before I would. I was clumsy with a cane, though. I had to walk slow and I still mixed up driveways, streets, and sidewalks. That can be very dangerous. That's when I decided to get a dog!

Lots of schools train dogs to help blind people. But only dogs trained at the Seeing Eye school in Morristown, New Jersey are called Seeing Eye dogs. The Seeing Eye school is America's oldest school for training dogs to guide people who are blind. They have the most experience. I wanted to go there. I didn't know much about dogs. I grew up in a house with six older brothers and sisters. There was no room for a dog. I was even a teeny bit afraid of dogs. But not anymore! Hanni and I are friends. We help each other, and we give each other confidence. I'm lucky to have her. She keeps me safe and sound.

B. Finke

Hanni and Beth: Safe & Sound *is available in braille from Seedlings Braille*
Books For Children: www.seedlings.org or 800-777-8552
Blue Marlin Publications is proud to donate a portion of the proceeds from the sales of this
book to Seedlings Braille Books For Children. To learn more about Seedlings Braille Books
For Children, and what you can do to help raise the literacy rate among children who are
blind, visit their site: www.seedlings.org

Braille Books For Children

"Placing a book in a child's hands is like planting a seed."

On-line Resources for Further Reading:

For more information about the Seeing Eye school, which raises and trains dogs like Hanni,
visit The Seeing Eye: **www.seeingeye.org**

For general information about guide dogs and guide dog schools across the United States,
visit Guide Dog Users Incorporated: **www.gdui.org**

To learn more about type 1 diabetes, which caused Beth's blindness, and a search for a cure,
visit The Juvenile Diabetes Research Foundation: **www.jdrf.org**

To learn more about blindness,
visit the following sites:
American Council of the Blind: **www.acb.org**
American Federation for the Blind: **www.afb.org**
National Federation of the Blind: **www.nfb.org**